DINOS

Have fun finishing the activities in this book!

*

Use the star stickers to celebrate as you complete each section.

*

You can use the other stickers wherever you want!

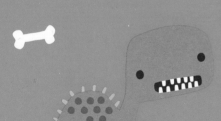

Silver Dolphin

Colorful Creatures

Make the dinosaurs look fun and colorful.

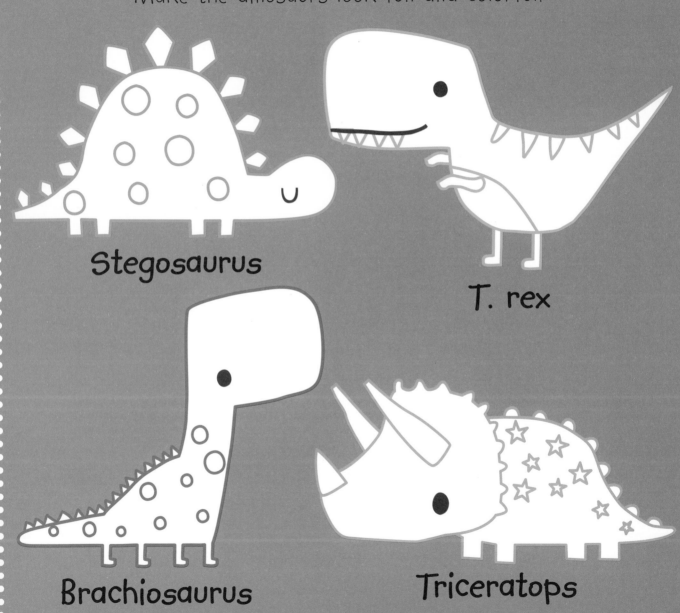

Stegosaurus

T. rex

Brachiosaurus

Triceratops

Hide-and-Seek

Search the scene. Circle the different dinosaurs.

Who has a bone? Who's dancing? Who has a bow?

Who has a donut? Who's brushing their teeth? Good job!

Find the Differences

Circle five differences between the scenes.

Good job!

Mix and Match

Draw lines from each baby dinosaur to its matching family.

blue baby

green baby

green family

red family

red baby

blue family

Color by Numbers

Use the key to color the picture.

Good job!

Dot-to-Dot

Connect the dots to see who's just hatched.

Dino Dash

Circle the one that's different in each row.

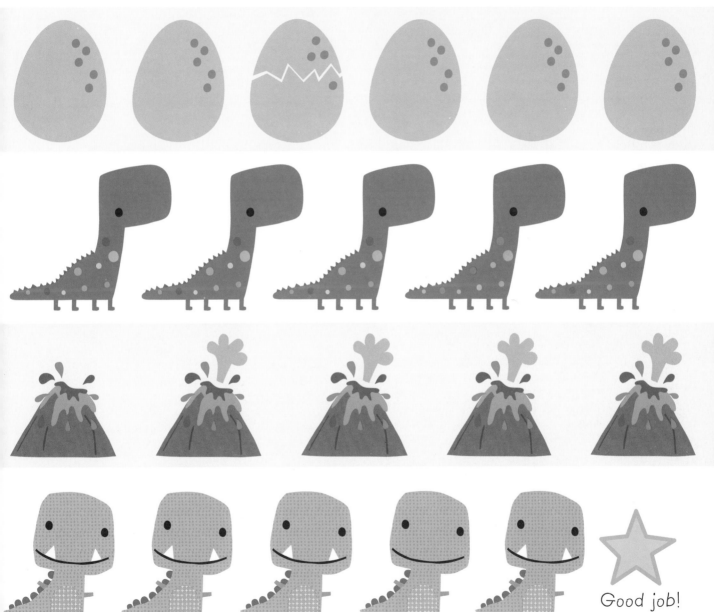

Good job!

Dino Maze

Guide the Parasaurolophus through the maze to reach her nest.

Start

Finish

Prehistoric Pictures

Color the hatching dinosaur
and decorate the eggs.

Good job!

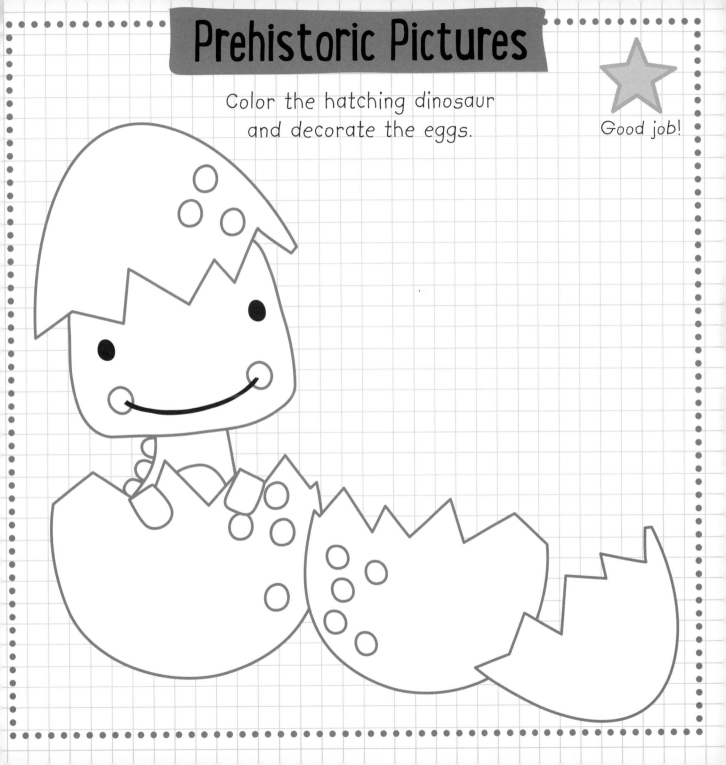

Colorful Creatures

Make the pictures look fun and colorful.

Pterodactyl

Ankylosaurus

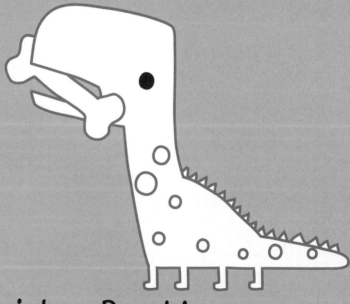

Paleontologist

Brachiosaurus

Hide-and-Seek

Search the scene. Circle the different pictures.

Who's hatching? Who's asleep? Whose wing is pink?

Who's lost their stripes? Who's wearing a flower?

Good job!

Find the Differences

Circle five differences between the scenes.

Good job!

Mix and Match

Count the creatures and draw lines from each number to the correct group.

1

Pterodactyls

3

Ankylosaurus

2

Velociraptors

Color by Numbers

Use the key to color the picture.

Good job!

1 2 3 4 5 6 7 8 9 10

Super Scene

Draw and sticker to finish the picture.

Good job!

Dot-to-Dot

Connect the dots to see who's dancing.

Dino Dash

Circle the one that's different in each row.

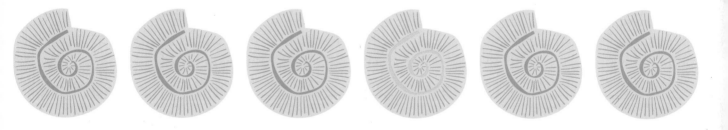

Good job!

Dino Maze

Guide the Brachiosaurus through the maze to reach his treats.

Start

Finish

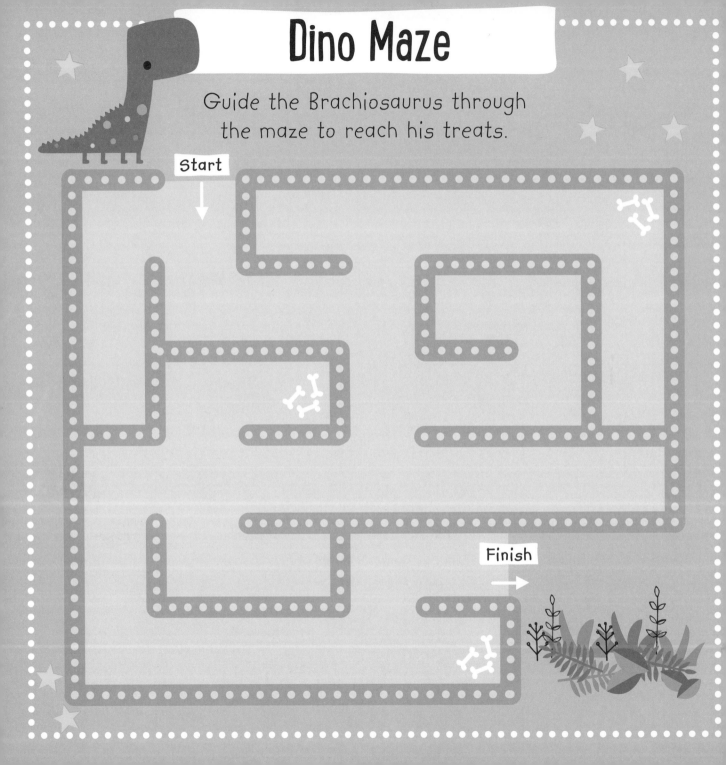

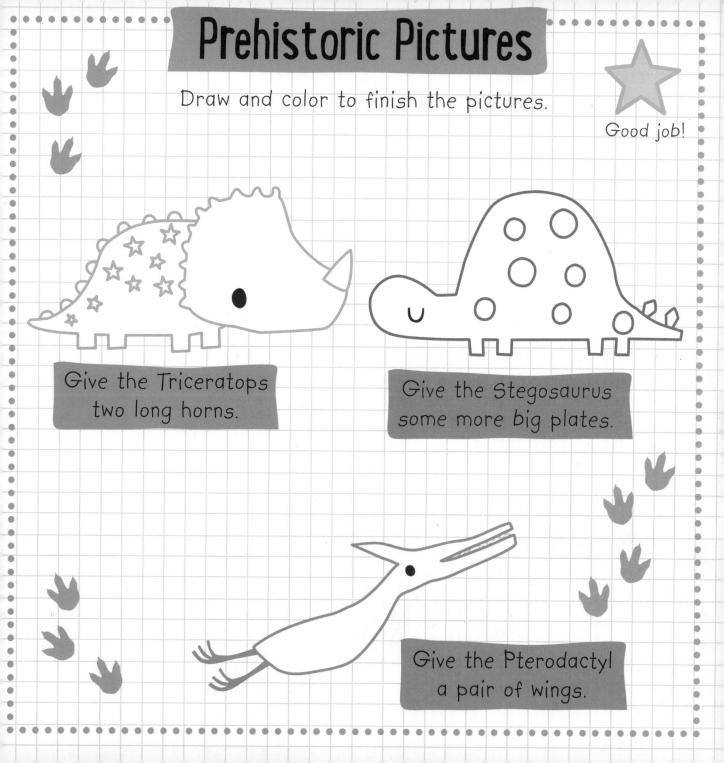

Prehistoric Pictures

Draw and color to finish the pictures.

Good job!

Give the Triceratops two long horns.

Give the Stegosaurus some more big plates.

Give the Pterodactyl a pair of wings.

Colorful Creatures

Make the dinosaurs look fun and colorful.

Velociraptor

Parasaurolophus

T. rex

Spinosaurus

Hide-and-Seek

Search the scene. Circle the different pictures.

What's turned pink? Who has a bag? Who has a shovel?

Which vehicle lost a wheel? Who lost their hat?

Good job!

Find the Differences

Circle five differences between the scenes.

Good job!

Mix and Match

Draw lines from each dinosaur to the matching colored egg.

orange
Spinosaurus

green egg

green
Triceratops

orange
egg

blue
Stegosaurus

blue egg

Color by Numbers

Use the key to color the picture.

Good job!

Dot-to-Dot

Connect the dots to see what the paleontologists have found.

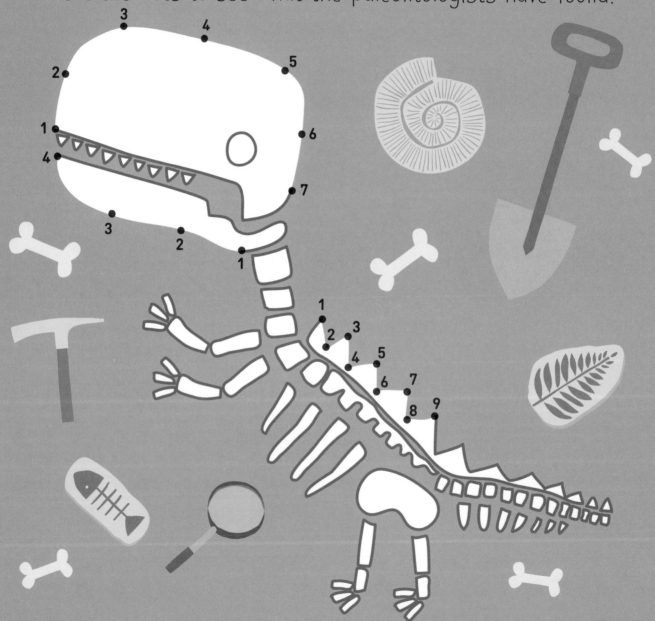

Dino Dash

Circle the one that's different in each row.

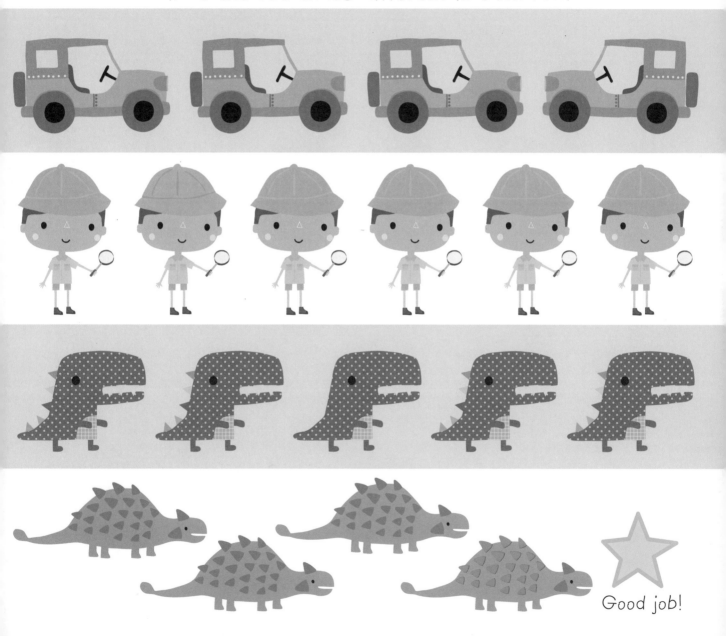

Good job!

Dino Maze

Guide the Velociraptor through the maze to reach his friends.

Start

Finish